HouseBeautiful

The
APARTMENT
BOOK

HouseBeautiful

The
APARTMENT
BOOK

Smart Decorating for Any Room—Large or Small

Carol Spier

HEARST BOOKS
New York

HEARST BOOKS
New York

An Imprint of Sterling Publishing
387 Park Avenue South
New York, NY 10016

Copyright © 2007 by Hearst Communications, Inc.
First Hardcover Edition 2012

Sterling ISBN: 978-1-58816-986-0

Book Design by Anna Christian

Library of Congress Cataloging-in-Publication Data

Spier, Carol.
 The apartment book : smart decorating for rooms small and large / Carol Spier
       p.cm.
Includes bibliographical references and index.
ISBN: 978-1-58816-986-0
 1. Apartments. 2. Interior decoration. I. Title.
NK2195.A6S65 2007
747'.88314—dc22

                        2006029559

Distributed in Canada by Sterling Publishing
C/o Canadian Manda Group, 165 Dufferin Street
Toronto, Ontario, Canada M6K 3H6
Distributed in Australia by Capricorn Link (Australia) Pty. Ltd.
P.O. Box 704, Windsor, NSW 2756, Australia

For information about custom editions, special sales, and premium and corporate purchases, please contact Sterling Special Sales at 800-805-5489 or specialsales@sterlingpublishing.com.

Manufactured in China

10 9 8 7 6 5 4 3 2 1

www.housebeautiful.com

contents

introduction

The classic quandary of how to make a house a home is as applicable to an apartment as it is to a freestanding residence. You probably know this if you are reading this book—you are or soon will be an apartment dweller—and you look forward to living in a space that is comfortable, convenient, attractive; a space filled with the style and ambiance you find appealing and reflective of you.

Small apartments may be smaller than a small house, but large ones rival grand houses in scale. So size is not really the difference between an apartment and a house; the limitations, advantages, and challenges of scale are the same in either. Ownership is not a difference either; you may own your coop or condo while others may rent a house. Apartment dwellers do have some unique issues and concerns: proximity to neighbors that brings concerns about privacy and noise; a limited number of exterior walls to offer windows for light and ventilation; a lack of control over building operation; shared mechanical systems; public hallways, elevators, and doormen. Residents of large buildings may be

Nest. One corner doubles as living and dining room in this tiny Manhattan apartment. Under the cloth is a fold-top table that moves aside so the owners can converse and relax on the armchair and banquette.

high above the street with great views and perhaps a balcony—hardly negatives! Loft dwellers enjoy large spaces, often only minimally divided—a plus for your sense of freedom, a minus when you're trying to create a bedroom and can't figure out how to bring natural light into the enclosure. And if you inhabit a studio apartment, chances are you're not only pressed for space, you're looking at everything you own no matter where you sit.

BASIC QUESTIONS GIVE YOU A SMART START

Begin your decorating plan by answering some basic questions: *Do you rent or own, and how long do you expect to live in the apartment?* The answer may affect the feasibility of major changes, or the size of the investment you make. *How old is your building, and what mechanical challenges will you face?* There may be structural, electrical, or plumbing restrictions or obstacles. *How accessible is your apartment?* Walk-ups are more awkward to update than first-floor or elevator-served apartments; building management, doormen, and superintendents may be friends or foes to workmen. *What kind of change do you want to make?* If it's just cosmetic, your task may be easy. If it's a gut and redo, how will you cope while the work is in process? *Will you plan the change yourself, or hire a designer?* However you answer this last query, the clearer your ideas for what you want to do are, the smoother the process will be and the better its results.

DREAM, DESIGN, DECORATE

The Apartment Book is filled with ideas for turning your apartment into your home. Six chapters devoted to individual rooms—Living Rooms, Dining Areas, Kitchens, Bathrooms, Bedrooms, and Foyers, Libraries, and Offices—feature hundreds of photographs of apartment interiors in every scale, decorated in many styles. You'll see terrific tiny kitchens, spacious lofts, modest living rooms, and grand dining rooms. Throughout the book are special features with ideas for solving common problems, like storage or the challenges of living in a small space, plus information and inspiration for displaying collections or using color. Tips are sprinkled among the photographs. Browse, read, and flag the photos that appeal to you. And be open—it's easy to pass over a good idea because you don't care for the style, color, or material used to execute it. Consider whether that shelf tucked below a kitchen window might be just the thing to solve your display problem before you dismiss it because you don't like stainless steel. The reverse is true too; you may fall in love with a color scheme used in a space that's nothing like yours. Take a look; you're sure to find a space that looks like home.

living rooms

Welcoming, relaxing, comfortable, gathering place. Your living room no doubt shares with the dining area the responsibility of being the most public part of your apartment—elegant or informal, expansive or intimate, it's a place where you entertain. When decorating it, your first goal is probably to provide comfortable seating arranged to invite conversation; with planning and an educated eye you can take that a step further and put together furnishings that share your hospitable spirit and reflect your taste in design and art.

Apartment living rooms come in all shapes and sizes, and while the challenges of decorating a small one differ from those for one that is grand, there are two steps that get any living room off to a good start: Choose a style that will give the ambiance you wish, and determine how to focus the layout. Your choice of style is mostly personal, but it could be guided by the architectural period of your apartment or by your locale. In addition, your style preference may depend on whether your apartment includes the luxury of a family room or den as well as a living room,

Purple passion. Making the most of every square foot, a cushioned banquette built into the corner opens up the floor space and provides hidden storage in this very small apartment. Rich, dense color on walls, floor, and accessories makes the tiny space feel delightfully enveloping and warm.

and whether children will frequent the room. Your choice of layout, on the other hand, is dependent on the configuration of the space—square or rectangular, large or small, as well as its relationship to other areas of the apartment—and on features such as a fireplace or view that you'd like to take advantage of, or an object such as a piano or large painting that is to be incorporated. There is probably more than one good way to arrange your furnishings, just think about the way the traffic will flow, whether conversation will be easy and facilitated by one or more groupings of furniture, and how natural and artificial lighting will come into play.

As you plan your decorating, review the questions in the Introduction; they'll help you understand the scope of your project and determine whether the work is a wise investment of time and resources for you as a renter or owner. Furniture can be moved with you or sold; paint, wallpaper, and built-ins cannot; and structural modification to your space adds another dimension to your project. Consider your responsibility as a neighbor, too: Are you taking proper steps to muffle your sound system? Will your window treatments shield neighbors from unwitting participation in your life?

As you look through the photos in this chapter you'll see many inviting options for living room design in both traditional and individual styles. Flag the ones that appeal to you. Make a list of your goals: a whole new look, a facelift, better reading light, a mural, a place to display your collection of ceramics. Read the special features: "Color Concepts," "10 Rules for Hanging Artwork," and "12 Tricks That Make Your Space Look Larger." Make a plan for creating your ideal living room, follow through with it, and live happily in your new space.

Virtuoso. A vibrant color mix calls for strong decorating. Bold patterns balancing blocks of solid hues and unlined silk taffeta curtains trimmed with box-pleated ruffles are brash, modern, and very American.

Pale harmony.
Stripped of its original paint, the carved stone mantel (above and opposite) shares the neutral palette of the other furnishings. The large mirror above it tosses light from the bank of windows across the space.

Timeless. Old and new mix comfortably in this updated classic city apartment. New half-walls and a mezzanine open onto the living room, where the original windows and mantel frame contemporary furnishings. Note the wide roller shade mounted at the ceiling.

Subtle and pretty. Above the dado, the walls are painted in a grid of perpendicular strié squares, and framed graphics hang at eye level, suspended from the crown molding. The soft, restful colors in this room are an elegant choice for the blend of old with new.

Social setting. An area carpet and luxuriously cushioned contemporary seating center a conversation area by the fireside in this living room, which is tall, narrow, and features the grand moldings typical of a period row house. A recamier in the bay window works for solitary relaxation or joins the group.

Visionary. This single room with elegant furnishings serves as living room, office, and formal bedroom; key to its success are the unconventional choice of melon as a neutral background, furniture chosen and arranged for socializing or privacy (the screen acts as bedroom wall), and an individualist use of pattern to loosen things up.

COLOR
CONCEPTS

COLOR CHANGES WITH THE LIGHT. When you choose specific paint hues and textiles or wallpaper, look at samples in your space under different lighting conditions. Wood, stone, and metal, of course, have color too. Surface plays a role as well: Reflective surfaces like glass or glazed tile make colors sparkle, absorbent surfaces like wood, honed stone, or velvet soften their effect.

PAINTED COLOR TRICKS:

- Moldings need not be painted a contrasting color. When architectural detail is elaborate (or moldings are in less-than-perfect condition), using one flat-finish color on everything may look elegant.
- Paint radiators to match the walls to make them less obtrusive.
- Use metallic paint to open up a long, dark hallway. Silvers and golds reflect light and make the space brighter.
- A painted ceiling influences ambiance without interrupting the eye—pink for warmth, sky blue for openness, midnight blue, silver, or gold for drama.
- One intensely colored wall in an all-white or neutral room will recede and add dimension to the space.

ACCESSORY COLOR TRICKS:

- Add colored lampshades; they can be custom-made from fabric or paper in almost any color imaginable.
- Use a colorful rug to enliven a drab or quiet room—it will ground the space and add depth and drama. Use a neutral rug to offset strong color elsewhere.
- Stretch a colorful quilt over an artist's canvas frame and hang it on a wall to add an instant shot of color.
- Frame a print with a mat that matches one of the artwork's dominant colors.
- Go for colorful slipcovers—they're not permanent, so you can change them to suit the season or a new mood.
- Pick one color to accent a monochrome décor, use it for pillows, a vase, a bowl, even fresh flowers—let your collection of yellowware, Jade-ite, or blue-and-white ceramics indicate the choice.
- Use one wonderfully multicolored textile or painting to set the palette for the room, repeating its hues individually on other furnishings.

COLOR SETS

TONE AND MOOD. Some decorating styles are associated with specific color palettes while others welcome the full spectrum. Color preference is personal—use color to express yourself.

Girly. Dubbed "the happiest place on earth" by the owner's boyfriend, this effervescent sitting room features lighthearted pretty colors, a deft mix of patterns, and contrasting soft and crisp lines.

To let your windows admit MAXIMUM LIGHT into a room, keep curtains as spare as possible.

Candy colors. Furniture resembling huge, bright pieces of candy sits in friendly anticipation of company in the grandly proportioned living room of this large loft. The unusual home office tucked in the corner is complementary and seems right at home.

Lightly punctuated. Lots of white and a mix of solid-color and simple graphic fabrics keep this traditionally furnished living room fresh and up-to-date. The grid arrangement of frameless paintings is arresting without being busy or overwhelming.

KARL BLOSSFELDT

SCHIRMER / MOSEL

Banish fussy window treatments from small rooms—hang simple panels or A CRISP ROMAN SHADE with a contrasting border.

Sitting pretty. Tailed white Roman shades edged in blue make jaunty toppers to the pair of windows at the end of this room. The wide, cushioned banquette below them conceals radiators and adds seating for good conversation or observation of the street scene outside.

Patchwork background. A tall folding screen covered in a tile-patterned fabric reiterates the colors, injects pattern into the square theme, and enhances the modernist furnishings.

Cube it. A modular unit opposite the sofa continues the square theme; it's fitted with rattan baskets for good-looking, easy pullout storage.

Proud to be square. This décor pays homage to the square in a palette of orange, brown, and ecru—even the square coffee table is copper-topped. The diagonal orientation of ceiling and rug pattern makes the room seem larger. Furnishings in solid-color fabrics, including the traditional curtains, keep the focus on the walls, floor, and ceiling.

SOLID COLOR UPHOLSTERY highlights the form of your furniture—prints call more attention to themselves than to the chair or sofa they cover.

Low profile. In a large room with a great view like this, low-slung furniture makes the vista outside the windows accessible from every corner and allows anyone sitting on the sofa to see the opposite interior spaces as well.

Wall art. The huge marble slab surrounding the fireplace is as important as a piece of artwork and provides the only pattern in the décor; the rug and upholstery are softly textured but solid-colored.

Nice touch. A mixture of textures—matte, slick, smooth, and nubby—and contrasting dark and pale colors add depth and interest to the clean lines of the furniture used in this sitting area. The huge mirror bounces light across the space. The leather armchair is a Hans Wegner Papa Bear wing chair from the 1950s.

Deep sheen. On the walls, a lacquered finish chosen for its light-reflecting qualities shows off a moody ultramarine hue, making it look rich rather than dark. The effect is complemented by the lustrous, inky velvet at the windows and on the upholstered pieces.

Atmospheric.
Furnishings in textured
taupes, browns, and grays
create shadows and depth
to bring a little mystery
to this previously "white
box" space.

Fuss free. Soaring proportions and linear
simplicity are the hallmarks of this living room,
which fills one corner of a duplex apartment. Long,
matching couches face one another on opposite
sides of the slate fireplace, which sits in handsome
relief against the one expanse of wall.

Show some leg—UNSKIRTED FURNITURE gives an illusion of depth. Skirted furniture closes off a space.

Spare symmetry. Open, floating shelves and a curtain of large plastic discs frame the sides of the sitting area in this large loft, giving it a sense of enclosure. The monochrome décor is marked by symmetry and a near-total absence of accessories or artwork; light and air take center stage.

Sliding walls. Window-like translucent panels separate this combination den and office from the adjacent living area; they keep light flowing and slide to provide privacy as needed. Built-in cupboards below the window abut the curved desk; the convex profile of the desk gives a larger surface, easier access to the view, and keeps anyone sitting there from feeling stuck in the corner.

Stylist. One room with balcony, overlooking park, with high ceiling and fireplace: Enviable components for studio apartments are here given a black-and-white palette, softened with grays and sepias and lightly accessorized with wire objects and containers that are decorative and functional.

10 RULES FOR HANGING ARTWORK

1.

BALANCE. Arranging photos and paintings is an art—the mix of proportions, texture, and color should look balanced of itself and in relation to the wall space and nearby furnishings. Work with a friend so one of you can hold the piece while the other appraises the effect.

2.

DENSITY HELPS. Hang photos or paintings close together to make the effect of the whole greater than the sum of the individual pieces.

3.

MOCK IT UP. Work out the relative positions in a group display by laying the pieces out on the floor.

4.

HOOK IT RIGHT. Hold a picture by the center of its wire and measure from the wire to the top of the frame; install the hanger so the bottom of the hook is that distance from the desired top of the picture.

5.

MIX THE MEDIA. It's okay for paintings, watercolors, prints, drawings, and photos to coexist in a single arrangement.

6.

FRAME A SERIES ALIKE. If the graphics are part of a series, or you want them to have a mass impact, use matching frames for all.

7.

FRAME TO SUIT. To avoid a mass-produced look and complement individual artworks, use a unique frame that suits each piece.

8.

GALLERY HALLWAY. Line a hallway or foyer with artwork to create a gallery—guests will pause to look instead of rushing through.

9.

MAKE SURE IT CAN BE SEEN. Choose eye-level display for smaller pieces, especially if they're hung individually.

10.

ALIGNMENT IS OPTIONAL. Framed photos and paintings need not be perfectly aligned on a wall. Choose a configuration that works with the architecture and other furnishings.

Two-in-one. The owners of this large apartment dedicated adjacent areas to formal and informal living, separating the two with sliding wood panels. When the panels are open, as here, both rooms seem larger; when closed, each is more intimate.

Inner sanctuary. The den adjacent to the formal living room seen above features a wall of open and enclosed shelves, which house books, stereo and a large television. Warm tones and comfortable furniture invite one to settle in and relax.

Reflection. Large, elegantly framed mirrors (one here behind the settee and another over the mantel, seen opposite) enlarge the space, reflecting the furnishings and giving the illusion of distant walls.

Mind your palette and proportions. The living room of this tiny Parisian apartment is lavishly furnished with elaborate period pieces. The limited palette, with lots of creamy white, gold, and a judicious use of green and rose, and the delicate proportions of the furniture and accessories are deftly combined to fill and flatter the very small room.

Lavender and luxe. A compelling mix of
furnishings from various decades of the twentieth
century makes this living room comfortable
and inviting. Believing a home should make the
residents look their best, the owner chose a palette
of lavender, soft gray, and gold that she feels is
especially flattering to her.

Window blessing. A window wall blesses this small, L-shaped studio with lots of light. The living and dining areas share the largest space; the sofa is turned away from the dining table to create some separation and faces a media cabinet placed against one wall (not visible here). In the foreground, a daybed with high head- and footboards creates an illusion of privacy in the sleeping ell.

Pastel haven. There's no pretense to large quarters here—it's one-room living, arranged with charm and focused on the marble period mantel. The small sofa doubles as footboard to the bed in the bow window, the chairs are intriguing, and a very contemporary freestanding closet has been tucked into the recess next to the fireplace.

12 TRICKS THAT MAKE YOUR SPACE LOOK LARGER

1.

CREATE PERSPECTIVES SO YOU DON'T FEEL CLOSED IN. The view from one room to another should be intentionally composed with a smooth transition from one ambiance to another.

2.

ROUND TABLES WORK WELL. They're easy to walk around and squeeze an extra chair up to. Plus they look fine if they're off center on a wall or in front of a sofa.

3.

GET RID OF DOORS WHEREVER YOU CAN. Replace them if you like with light curtains—funky ones made of light-bulb pull chains or colorful strung beads could be just the thing.

4.

MIRRORS OPEN UP SMALL SPACES. Many mirrors set at different angles open up a room and reflect bits and pieces of things you might not otherwise notice.

5.

LATERAL ACCENTS EXPAND THE SPACE. Paint your walls with horizontal bands in three related colors or several sheens of the same hue.

6.

USE MANY SMALL SOURCES OF LIGHT. Lampshades that concentrate the light give the impression that a space is larger.

7.

LEAVE THE CEILING UNLIGHTED OR YOU'LL FEEL IT'S ON YOUR HEAD. Several small lamps will add character and depth to the room.

8.

ADD INTERIOR WINDOWS. Open spaces in a wall allow light, air, and conversation to pass from room to room.

9.

KEEP THE EYE MOVING. Make window treatments and walls the same color.

10.

GO FOR THINGS OF GOOD QUALITY. In a small space everything gets noticed.

11.

USE LIGHT FURNITURE WITH LEGS. Skirted furniture takes up more visual room and closes up a space.

12.

DECORATE WITH INTENTION. Haphazard décor just accentuates the shoebox effect typical of a small space.

Classy comfort. A balance of uptown and downtown sensibilities that includes a soft ivory, green, and earth-tone palette, luxe velvet and simple linen, and a mix of mid-century American, Chinese, and Louis XVI pieces—juxtaposed as if they're having a conversation—gives this living room its particular harmonious charm. The corner banquette makes great use of what could have been a problem corner between the doorway and fireplace.

A NEUTRAL PALETTE helps create a serene environment.

New meets old. Modern furnishings work just as well as traditional ones would in this room, which has elegant architectural details. Easing the blend of old with new styles are contemporary informal chandeliers and a uniform soft white background.

Color definition. A long room containing both the living and dining areas seems even longer thanks to the mirror at the far end. A neutral palette keeps the room relaxed, while the glass lamp bases add touches of shimmer around the space. The dark color of the dining chairs and the frame around the mirror add a bit of strong contrast, setting the dining area apart.

Harmonized. An area carpet stops short of two structural columns to define and contain the sitting space in this loft; from the sofa, the columns frame the dining area beyond an interior passage.

Brilliant colorist. A gutsy mix of lime green, peacock, violet, and golden yellow makes traditional pieces look fresh. The white walls setting them off here have been textured with fluted plaster, giving an architectural presence to the room.

MONOCHROMATIC COLOR SCHEMES are a great decorating device—to be most effective, they need at least three shades of the same color.

Shimmery walls. Glowing gold and verdigris tones create a rich backdrop to this small, high-ceilinged seating area. Gray, black, and honey-colored furnishings fit calmly into this space. The piecing of the full-length curtains introduces a horizontal element, a nice balance for the overall proportions.

Matte and shiny. Clean lines, rich but low-key colors, and just a few striking accessories complement this raised hearth of polished stone slabs, which is juxtaposed with a fireplace surround of stacked, natural stone and commands the stage in this contemporary living room.

Sharp angle.
A diagonal arrangement allows a fair number of boxy pieces to sit lightly in this small square room. The lamp introduces additional diagonals while the tubular metal armchairs keep the space feeling open. The easel makes a fine support for framed artwork where there is no wall.

Out of Africa. A witty blend of traditional and exotic tastes sets the tone in this small apartment, where elegant furnishings sit between indigo zebra-stripe wallpaper and woven bamboo matting. The furniture is small in scale as befits the space and the textiles kept quite plain to relieve the vibrant, busy background.

Mirror, mirror. Opposite the sofa, a fireplace is flanked by tall, indigo bookcases. A mirrored wall around it opens up this end of the room; it is topped with a second, large, gilt-framed mirror—a nice detail that brings a period touch to a modern convention.

Color classic. Rooms decorated in blue and white always seem fresh and crisp. Here the colors define the sitting area centered in a large, multipurpose room. The informal coffee table is a camp bed with a striped mattress.

Individualist. Fearless pink walls declare this to be a very personal space put together by someone with an unerring eye for color, which makes possible a successful mix of such eclectic furnishings in an architecturally grand and formal room.

Red surround. Deeply colored walls—often in red or green hues—are traditional choices when intimacy is the desired effect in a living room, den, or library. Here, a highly glazed, red-on-red ragged finish is cheery when reflecting sunlight and turns cozy when the curtains are pulled and lamplight glows.

Easy whites. Natural wood tones and white make an easy backdrop; if the furniture is also white, you'll find that even a bit of color really pops. The décor here is simple and comfortable, the bouquet and rose-colored pillows warm it up.

Light and dark. With the chimneypiece painted white to match the walls, this mantel disappears while the objects on it come into focus. The dark hearth and firewall are balanced by the cordovan leather chair, while the red lamp base stands brightly on a dark side table.

Flower power. With its bold prints, modern art, and a palette inspired by the throw pillows—covered in a contemporary take on an eighteenth-century flame-stitch pattern—this sitting room is totally today. The walls are covered in handwoven raffia that reads as denim. When the large bolsters are removed, the sofa reveals its true colors as a guest bed.

ELIOT PORTER *Photographs and text by Eliot Porter*

SLIM AARONS · ONCE UPON A TIME

TWINS MARY ELLEN MARK

Two-tone comfort. Dark colors and invitingly plump, oversize pieces taking a lot of space are an unexpected solution to the challenge of a small living room. This design is very efficient—you can settle in to relax and even dine—and the large mirror, light walls, and full-length curtains set off and soften the black.

Poet's corner. A window recess, square area rug, and L-shaped sofa define the sitting room in one corner of this large open room and a pale palette reinforces the spaciousness. Note how the exposed cabinet at one end of the sofa provides great display space and balances the slight asymmetry of the setup.

BEFORE AND AFTER

Opened and Updated

BEFORE
Dark floors and heavy drapes made this living room seem dark despite the two big windows at the end. Although a large space, it felt closed in to the owner, who disliked its isolation from the rest of the apartment. In fact, the chief drawback of the apartment was its layout—the only entry to any room was through an interior hall.

AFTER
In a triumph of demolition that dispelled the room's cavernous feeling, nearly half the wall between the living room and adjacent dining room was knocked down and replaced with a sliding, translucent door. Now both spaces share the light from their windows, and people and conversation move freely from one room to the next.

1. The dividing door slides into a pocket in the wall, so it disappears when fully open. When closed, light still passes through it.

2. The windows once blocked by draperies are now veiled with solar shades, which let the sunlight in while minimizing glare and maintaining the view.

3. To bridge the change in level between the two rooms, a broad step was added below the sliding door.

4. Simple lines and a palette of light, neutral tones make the furnishings appear to float in the airy space.

5. Steel radiator covers, now stripped and burnished, pay a nice compliment to the sliding-door frame. They're topped by a long maple shelf, which spans the room.

You'll never be wrong to embellish your living room with **A VASE OF FRESH FLOWERS**. Or if you have natural light, use a large potted plant.

Patterned accent. At first glance Bohemian chic seems to rule this atelier/living space, but a second look reveals that the use of pattern, while important, is fairly restrained. The mirrored folding screen gives focus to the corner sitting area and makes all the details wonderful—three times over.

Sunny invitation. Daylight enters this inviting spot from the wall opposite the armoire, filling the room with sunshine. The armoire is a bar, hence the adjacent shelves stocked with glasses. The nineteenth-century mirror frames above the sofa are a combination of studded leather and wood.

Bookish. This booklover's sitting room has terrific full-length windows, which make it seem larger than it is. The angled seating brings guests together for a tête-à-tête; solid color upholstery gives each piece a modern poise despite the assorted period styles.

Seeing double. A big mirror leaning against the wall captures filtered sunlight and adds a charming background to this end of the room. The ottoman can double as a coffee table.

Art first. A large painting on one wall dominates this loft living area. The furnishings echo its cinnamon and brown tones and the carpet offers the only other pattern. The arrangement of the seating pieces keeps eyes focused on the art and permits easy access to it.

Graphic backdrop. A large map, cut up and mounted in a grid of individually framed sections, fills the space above the plain shelves at the end of this small sitting area. Its dusky monotone and visual texture are fine complements to the handsome taupe, gray, and yellow room.

Open space. Although centered on the window and in its space, this furniture arrangement has a pleasant asymmetry, designed to showcase the single piece of art that fills the wall behind the side chairs. The floor cushion provides extra seating while keeping the room open to the adjacent area.

Mellow tones.
The taupe and honey tones of the walls and furnishings complement the smoky, reflective surface of the art that commands this room.

Art patron. This sitting area is one end of a great room, used by the family to watch TV (hidden behind the wall panels), relax, and read. The rich tones, simple lines, and varied textures of the furnishings mitigate any feeling of austerity and play an intentionally supporting role to the art.

All lined up. A substantial frame anchors the graphic centered over this sofa; a small, delicate molding would be out of scale in this setting. The row of snapshots tacked below is fun and fits neatly in its space.

Oversize paintings open up
a room, CREATING A VISTA or
second window—especially if
there is no view.

Put in proportion. Oversized to the point of nearly dwarfing its surroundings, this artwork is perfectly balanced in its space and claims the attention it deserves—larger furniture would be out of scale and spoil the effect.

A tautly upholstered, solid-color sofa flanked by STANDING LAMPS helps a petite living room to appear expansive.

Symmetrical to a point. Symmetrical arrangements are satisfying, and the less rigid the mirroring, the livelier they are. With fun colors, witty patterns, and a rather offbeat style mix, this setup delights the eye. The small shades on the floor lamps provide just the right fill for the spaces between the painting and the mismatched end tables.

Off-center. Asymmetrical arrangements invite the eye to travel rather than focus on a central point. This one is well balanced and leads you on a diagonal journey from the blue square on the right side of the painting to the bolster and then up to the small figure on the tall post or down to the lower blue pedestal.

Framed reflection. This mirror is the same width as the settee beneath it and fills the classic role of a large mirror—it makes the small room seem larger and brighter, and being handsomely framed, is decorative in its own right.

Eye-catcher. Sparkling like a marvelous giant brooch pinned above the sofa, this elaborate mirrored frame demands attention. Unlike a large framed mirror, it doesn't reflect and expand the space—its role is to dazzle and intrigue.

Bohemian. Bookshelves rim the perimeter of this duplex loft, where old and modern mix stylishly and various seating groups play host individually or as a group. Pilasters framing the shelf bays echo the columns that punctuate the space—both shelves and pilaster capitals are neatly fitted under the stairs.

Hall with one wall. Here, a hallway of sorts exists between the table-backed sofa and the painting hung opposite it, effectively dividing a large open space into two separate seating areas. The wall at the end of this passage has been fitted with discreet shelves (one at table height) while the table behind the sofa gives a sense of purpose to the walkway.

Neat retreat. This small space has been set up as a den; there is just room for a coffee table between the sofa on one wall and the modular shelves on the other. The bookshelf tower on the end wall balances the wood panel on the left of the window; together they frame a cabinet that hides the heat duct.

If you can't afford to install built-in cabinetry to create STREAMLINED ORGANIZATION, try lining up several tall bookcases.

Open and shut. The thoughtfully designed built-in storage unit serves as an unobtrusive media wall in the den on the facing page. The strategic combination of open cubes, sliding doors, and assorted drawers is both handy and good-looking.

dining areas

Inviting, festive, relaxing, elegant and informal by turns. Whether you have a dining room, dining area, or a table in a nook that does double duty as desk, the place where you dine should be welcoming and comfortable. The layout of your apartment and the way you live and entertain influence the way you decorate your dining room: If it's used for breakfast, lunch, and dinner you'll furnish it differently from one reserved for formal entertaining; and if your dining area is part of a large living space you'll have different, and limited, options for its design. Unless you reserve your dining room for formal entertaining, chances are you want it to be flexible, so take advantage of the versatility inherent in dining décor and use a variety of linens and tableware to give it different looks, and change the ambiance with candlelight, a chandelier, sconces, or sunlight.

Stand in the doorway or at the edge of your dining space and think about its configuration, proportions, and architectural features. Is the ceiling high or low? Where are the windows? Is there a fireplace? Is the space intimate or grand? Think about how you use it: Does it house your

Dreamscape. Walls lacquered in pale aqua create an oasis of calm in this dining room. The table is finished to look like inlaid ivory, and on the wall, celadon vases on small plaster brackets surround an exotic mirror.

library, and is artwork important to the décor? Do you host buffets or serve at the table? If it is not a separate room, how do you want to define it within the larger space? Is it an alcove? And are there columns, a raised or sunken area, a counter on which to center it? Or is the space so open that simply placing the table and chairs creates a dining area; and if so, what else happens in the space, and what is the best way to accommodate its other functions and optimize the flow from one to another? Or is the space so small that you're not quite sure you even have a dining area?

However the nature and size of your dining area affect the way you set it up, your enjoyment of it will center on the table and chairs that welcome you to good food and conversation; and their proportion to the room is critical—too large and the effect will be crowded or clumsy, too small and the dining area will look lonely. Consider not only the visual proportions; if your space is small, make sure there is room to pull chairs away from the table or pass behind seated diners to serve or clear the table.

To begin your decorating plan, answer the basic questions given in the Introduction. You'll gain some insight about the scope of your project and, especially if you are considering structural changes, be able to judge whether your plan makes sense for you as a renter or owner. Then gather your design ideas—you'll find lots of inspiration for all kinds of dining areas in the photos in this chapter. Be sure to read the special features, "Well Lit" and "10 Ways to Show Off a Collection." Make your choices and drink a toast to your new dining room.

Panoply of greens. A mix of forest green, olive green, and moss green hues gives this dining area a bright, fresh, lush look that's heightened by the matte-and-shiny striped curtains, large-scale grass-pattern tablecloth, and vivid painting. Touches of white and hot pink accent the palette, and chairs with curvy backs contrast and soften the rectilinear architecture.

Bon appétit. In a dining room filled with family heirlooms, elegant furnishings and glittering crystal are tempered by brown Venetian plaster walls, which look like suede, a device that softens the ambiance and showcases artwork. Matte lavender cotton covering the chairs balances the gleam of the ebony table.

Game plan. When dinner is just for two in this apartment that lacks a dining room, a folding game table in front of the living room bookshelf holds the repast. When the occupants give a dinner party, they pull chairs up to a library table on another side of the room.

Step up to the plate. A floor level change of one, two, or more steps provides an instant division of the space in an apartment layout, creating a mezzanine effect, which here separates and defines the dining area without closing it off from the living room.

Contemporary craft. If you want to minimize the distinction between the spaces in a loft, choose table, chairs, sofa, coffee table, and easy chairs that share a design aesthetic—but don't be afraid of pieces with character. This unusual table adds visual texture and complements the overall use of clean lines and rich neutral hues against pale walls and draperies.

WELL
LIT

EVERY ROOM NEEDS THREE KINDS OF LIGHTING: *natural* (from a window), *ambient* (from overhead fixtures and wall sconces), and *task* (from fixtures focused on a work or reading area; lighting for artwork or a hall table falls into this category). Dimmer controls allow you to adjust ambient light. Flexible-arm or otherwise-adjustable fixtures are an enhancement for task lighting.

IN AN OPEN-PLAN LAYOUT, a good lighting design will help create "rooms" where there are no walls.

LIGHT CAN BE WARM OR COOL and affects the color and mood of the things it touches. The temperature of natural light varies with exposure (east, west, north, or south), time of day, and neighboring surroundings such as overhanging eaves, trees, or nearby buildings. The temperature of artificial light can be controlled by the kind of light bulb you use, and is also affected by the color of the lampshade.

LIGHTING DESIGN IS COMPLEX. Seek professional help if you don't know what to do (and most of us don't), especially if you are renovating a space. And if a fixture doesn't simply plug in, hire an electrician to install it legally and safely.

LAMPSHADES ARE NOT ONE-SIZE-FITS-ALL. Take your lamp with you when purchasing a shade. And don't be shy if you don't see what you want, many vendors can arrange to have shades custom-made.

STYLE IS A MATTER OF TASTE. Modern light fixtures are wonderfully adaptive and look good with many styles of architecture and furnishings. You needn't be hung up on tradition—choose fixtures for the way their scale and materials fit with your other furnishings, as well as for their design lines.

FIGURE LIGHTING FIXTURES INTO YOUR BUDGET. While you may find the perfect (and perfectly priced) pendant, floor, or table lamp at the thrift shop or a trendy home store, the fixtures you really want may require an investment. Plan ahead for them—it's a shame to spoil a good decorating scheme with lamps purchased as an afterthought.

Table for two. The dining area in a small, open-plan apartment is often by default just any spot a table will fit. This one successfully sits between kitchen and living areas, with a single color scheme of pale wood, white, glass, and dusty green unifying the spaces. The round table can be moved farther into the room to accommodate a few guests.

Grand reflection. An enormous mirror tricks the eye into perceiving this dining area at twice its actual size. Dining chairs in three styles around the mahogany and stainless-steel table introduce variety to the simple décor; a shared palette keeps the effect harmonious. Note the fabrics on the chairs—the slipcover is made of wool with a skirt of linen gauze.

Chocolate wrapper. Walls painted a deep bittersweet chocolate hue create a sense of intimacy in this tall, imposing room. While a light color might be severe in a room this size, the dark color works well with the blue-and-white and gilt furnishings and looks lovely in candlelight. Dinner for 16 is not on the owner's schedule, so rather than waste the space as a formal dining room he'd never use, he set it up as a combination sitting-dining room, where coffee and conversation can be served at the sofa.

> To give the ILLUSION OF HEIGHT, hang curtains from poles mounted as close to the ceiling as possible.

Gather round. A round table will usually feel less cumbersome than a square one in a small space. The ornate pedestal makes this handsome example a stylish choice for a dual library- and dining-table role, and despite its mass, it sits comfortably in its corner.

Tête-à-tête. There's no better invitation to intimate dining than a table for two in front of a fireplace— especially in a small space that's decorated in a personal manner. Here, walls have been draped with flat panels of white canvas, which accentuate an eclectic collection of furnishings.

Take tea. With a wall of shelves as backdrop, this seating group invites discussion of a good book or hosts an intimate tea party. Sconces on the shelf casing illuminate the books, display, and loveseat.

Striped hangout. A "great room" it may not be, but this combination living/library/dining area, which opens from a kitchen to the left, serves the same purpose. Family life centers here happily, if compactly, and the cook is never isolated. The broad horizontal stripes on the wall keep your eye moving around the small space.

Terrace effect. Count an alcove with French doors as an architectural blessing that will grace many a meal. Sunny colors and ornamental metal grilles create a Mediterranean ambiance, but whatever style of furnishings you choose, you can't go wrong with a setting like this one.

Corner built-in. An upholstered, high-backed banquette provides comfortable seating that saves space in a tight spot. This one matches the wall to keep its corner looking as large as possible; a tiny pedestal table and generously matted artwork complete the uncluttered design.

> A niche built into a wall FUNCTIONS LIKE A WINDOW if it holds a painting, sculpture, or large textile—you'll perceive the display as a view.

Lofty lifestyle. If your space has assorted wall surfaces like the brick and wallboard in this loft, acknowledge them when you hang artwork. The white wall offers a clean background; its nicely designed niche adds a subtle frame to a display of objects as well as a portrait. The brick is busy; the abstract painting is at once a strong accent and the perfect complement to its texture.

Shades of red. Here, an all-white paint treatment minimizes a plethora of moldings and calms the walls, which form a backdrop for works of art and the tall lamps that frame the clean lines of the sideboard and dining table. The composition is punctuated with graphic red lampshades that lead the eye to the painting.

Small and detailed. A tiny dining area, thoughtfully designed, can be as inviting as one that's grand. A corner banquette with soft cushions, a handsome table and chairs, one large print centered behind the table, and charming display nooks high above all make this a delightful place to sup.

Nice curves. This graceful modern table and playfully colored chairs are visually light yet strong enough to look balanced in this space with a very high ceiling. The long, low-arch table is an amusing counterpoint to the more classically proportioned archway that leads from the neighboring room.

BEFORE AND AFTER

Properly Proportioned

AFTER

A neutral palette and furnishings with stature move the room into the modern world. Gone are the fussy carpet, delicate period dining set, slipcovered casual chair, and vivid blue ceiling. The new look is serene, uncluttered, and refined yet not overly formal.

1. Above the picture rail, vertical-stripe wallpaper (interesting and, unlike the pictures previously there, easily understood from below) lifts the eye to the ceiling.

2. The ceiling recesses are now a pale, restful taupe.

3. The pendant light fixture and sconces are graphic, simple, and appropriately proportioned for the large room.

4. Artwork is centered on the panels and hung at eye level for greater impact and appreciation.

5. Upholstered chairs and a table with heft hold their own against the moldings.

6. A textured, solid color carpet echoes the creamy tones of the walls and ceiling and sets off the darker tones of the table and chairs.

BEFORE

This dining room has great architectural details but its original décor felt haphazard and a bit stodgy to the young couple who own it. The look was cluttered, the easy chair was out of place, and the artwork lost atop the picture rail. But good news—the challenge here was cosmetic, no structural changes were in order.

Ensemble impact. Against white walls and a built-in cabinet that matches the floor, and with accessories kept to a minimum, the full sculptural impact of this mahogany table and chairs is immediately apparent. The robin's egg blue door is a whimsical piece of the apartment owner's art collection.

Invisible chairs. The floor plan in this uptown Manhattan apartment has been opened up for a loft-like effect, with living, dining, and kitchen areas leading one to another. The lacquered-oak dining table is here fully expanded for entertaining, surrounded by transparent chairs that nearly disappear to keep the space visually open and uncluttered.

Kitchen partner. An orange table runner adds a splash of color and texture to this dining area. Stylish white chairs paired with a dark table make a clean and modern composition that segues nicely to the adjacent kitchen and is as perfect for family meals as for entertaining guests.

Furnishings come sharply into focus in spare, spacious rooms, so choose pieces with strong design lines, ASSERTIVE COLORS, or sculptural qualities.

Surface appeal. Enliven a neutral or monochromatic color scheme with an assortment of textures—the effect is quieter than a mix of patterns yet still interesting. Here, the wire open-weave chairs complement the rough brick wall and metal radiator, the polished table is balanced by the sheen of the mirror, and the carpet and blinds each add a bit of dimension.

10 WAYS TO SHOW OFF A COLLECTION

1.

GROUP IT. For impact, separate items into small groupings of roughly equal mass, then arrange the groupings on a set of shelves.

2.

STACK THEM. If you collect items with flat tops, place them one atop another, making several short towers; then arrange the towers on a shelf, console, or bench.

3.

CHOOSE THE RIGHT BACKGROUND. Pick a color for the wall, cupboard, or case that complements and contrasts the color of your collection, or create an intentionally monochrome display.

4.

BE A COPYCAT. Look in magazine, boutiques, and museums for display ideas; adapt them to your décor.

5.

CONTAIN SMALL ITEMS. Little treasures will be lost and swallowed in large areas. Arrange them on a tray, in a bowl, a curio cabinet, or another defined space.

6.

FIND A RHYTHM. Analyze the details of shape, pattern, or color in your collection; arrange items so these details alternate, mirror, or sit in rows in a pleasing way.

7.

LAYER WITH CARE. When placing numerous items on a deep shelf, put larger pieces toward the back and overlap with smaller ones in front—so that each can be appreciated.

8.

LIGHT IT. Make sure there is appropriate illumination for your treasures to be appreciated by both day and night. Also protect them from direct sunlight.

9.

CONSIDER PROPORTION. If one piece in your collection is much larger than the others, let it be the center of your display.

10.

SHOW THEM OUT OF CONTEXT. Themed collections take on fresh meaning and gain sculptural impact if they're displayed in a room other than the one they'd normally be used in.

Urbane. Multipaned cast-iron windows give a sense of enclosure and coziness to this Manhattan dining room. Enhancing the effect are pale yellow iridescent curtains that make you feel the sun is always shining through the window. Neutral walls and furnishings set up a contemporary but timeless mood and showcase the Asian antiquities collected by the owner.

Individualist. In this small dining room an ebonized finish on the armoire, table, and chairs adds depth and gloss that contrast the texture of the baskets, carpet, metal lantern, and collections. The hand-tying on the backs of the dining chairs is so beautiful the owner chose to leave it exposed so he can enjoy the texture it adds to the mix.

An OPEN ARMOIRE is more interesting than a closed one. Invite people to look into your secret world.

kitchens

Efficient, up-to-date, inviting, roomy, the heart of the home. Fortunate are those who have such a kitchen, and who among us doesn't want one that meets this description? Apartment dwellers are often faced with kitchens that are small, bland, old, or isolated; but imagination and good planning can make this sort of unsatisfactory room welcoming and a pleasure to use, no matter its size or the size of your budget. In fact, a kitchen that looks perfect at first glance may be more of a challenge to make your own than one that's obviously problematic—you may not recognize the things that make it wrong for you or may be reluctant to invest time or money altering something so apparently fine.

A well-designed kitchen—regardless of dimension, style, or budget—has the best possible arrangement of work space and appliances, organized, efficient storage, good lighting, and a personal ambiance. Of course, when it comes to space, more is almost always truly more in a kitchen; but if you accept reality, define your needs, and do some creative problem-solving, you can achieve very good—even perfect—results whatever the scale of your update.

Gem kitchen. A strong brush of emerald-green paint with a lacquered finish brought excitement to the existing laminate cabinets and a roller shade in this city kitchen, in which, despite its small footprint, the occupants have no trouble cooking for eight.

Begin by answering the questions given in the Introduction—a reality check about the wisdom of investing in the apartment and the feasibility of making physical changes, not only to walls but also to plumbing and wiring, is especially important for kitchen updates, which can be both costly and disruptive. Your answers will give you some perspective on the scope of the project ahead of you, whether it's a simple reorganization of the cabinets, a cosmetic makeover with fresh paint and hardware, a moderate renovation, or a complete gut and rebuild.

Next, move to the fun part and put together a plan. Gather your thoughts and ideas. List the challenges you face, the problems you want to solve, and the things you dislike about the kitchen as it is. Collect visual references for the way you want the kitchen to be. Don't confuse style with ideas: A counter or shelf cleverly fitted in an odd space, a great configuration of appliances, or a marvelously organized cupboard may be perfect for you once you look beyond materials or colors that are not to your taste. Go shopping to see options for whatever you plan to add. Ask questions of vendors and also of friends who have gear you like. Two things especially important—and easily overlooked—in an apartment kitchen are the exhaust system for the stove, because exterior walls may not be accessible, and the operating noise of appliances, which may permeate not only your space but your neighbors' as well.

The pages that follow feature apartment kitchens sized from almost unimaginably tiny to luxuriously large. You'll see that even a small room can feel open and nice to work in, if not exactly spacious, and will find aesthetics that range from quirky to retro to classic to very modern, from informal to professional. Check out the special features, "9 Ways to Make the Most of Kitchen Storage" and "10 Details That Make a Small Kitchen Great." Enjoy your perfect kitchen.

A place for everything. White-in-white open storage tucked between two windows keeps dishes handy and forms a textured background to this kitchen workspace. Below the shelves a mirrored backsplash gives a clean reflection that masquerades as a space-expanding pass-through. Countertops made of recycled glass and mother-of-pearl are durable, practical, and environmentally responsible, plus they sparkle appealingly.

> Honed stone countertops are softer to the touch and **LESS REFLECTIVE** than polished ones.

Gallery kitchen. It can be challenging to integrate kitchen furnishings with adjacent living spaces in a loft. In this instance, cabinets topped by a counter with a high backsplash are handsome, and large photographs replace upper cabinets (which wouldn't fit in front of the end window anyway) and provide continuity with those in the next room.

Simple pleasures. Understated design with every detail thoughtfully chosen works well and looks smart in small kitchens. This space couldn't be simpler, yet the white cabinets, farmhouse sink with elegant faucet, soapstone counters, and white subway tile make an appealing and detailed composition.

Classy whites. This renovated Manhattan kitchen displays the contemporary face of a classic prewar design that has just enough space for a breakfast table and chairs. The pattern of the Calacatta Gold marble backsplash adds interest to the all-white palette, as does the grid on the cabinetry, a detail borrowed from the divided-light cast-iron windows. Antique Chinese bamboo chairs add a warm tone and are similarly geometric.

Decent exposure. Vanilla tones on walls and cabinets (refrigerator door panels included), chrome hardware, and white marble countertops keep the atmosphere open. Glass doors reflect light but they also display their contents, so think of what is inside your cabinets before fronting them transparently.

Kitchen lab. Industrial metal shelving provides sturdy, flexible storage and keeps the upper half of this kitchen more open than cabinets would. It's a nice complement to the stainless-steel refrigerator too.

Small luxuries. Stainless appliances like this stove and exhaust hood look sleek and professional, whether commercial or conventional in scale. Note two simple luxuries here: a niche below the hood to keep condiments and other necessaries handy, and a built-out backsplash below the window for display or storage.

BEFORE AND AFTER

Small Can Be Beautiful

AFTER

Determined to make room for counters along both sides of the room, the owner bravely demolished the plumbing wall and moved it back about 18 inches. This eliminated the odd space next to the radiator, created a recess for cabinets and counter, and allowed for a bench in the newly opened span below the window. The stove was replaced and relocated to the opposite side of the room.

1. Contemporary adjustable track lighting can be focused where needed and looks nifty.

2. Glass-fronted upper cabinets stop short of the window to keep the space feeling open. There are narrow open shelves at their end.

3. The handy raised shelf on the counter provides handsome camouflage for the original plumbing stack; there's a flue for the pipes inside the cabinets.

4. An undermounted sink looks sleek and uncluttered—plus, one swipe with a sponge sends drips and spills into it.

5. The top of the bench is flush with the radiator cover, creating a deep windowsill and extending to the left as a narrow shelf.

6. A small round table on wheels scoots easily aside for access to the bench. Its wire legs keep it from looking heavy or awkward.

BEFORE

Depressing is hardly the word for this 1936 kitchen, which was in worse than original state. The tiny room was dark, dreary, and had virtually no counterspace. There was nowhere to sit nor room for a table—just an awkward, useless space between the range and window—and the exhaust fan with airborne cord was definitely not a plus.

A BOTTOM-DRAWER FREEZER
compartment saves wear on your
back because the refrigerator,
which you open more frequently,
will be easier to access.

Mix metaphors. Credenza-like Euro-style cabinets are modern classics with a proper solidity that makes them a good, if unexpected, fit for an apartment with stately prewar architecture. Sitting on slender legs as they do, the base cabinets are easy to clean under too.

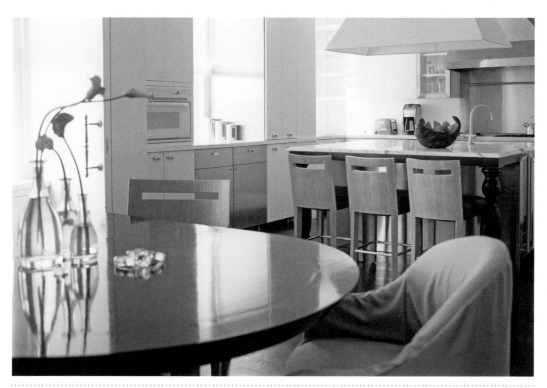

Invite mingling. A kitchen that is wide open to the dining area allows cooks and diners to interact. Here, a breakfast bar that can double as a buffet also provides work space, making up for counter area given over to the deep cabinets adjacent to the windows. The white cabinets are punctuated occasionally with stainless steel ones, creating sleek contrast.

Every quarter-inch counts. This kitchen is barely larger than a closet yet it is so well planned that dinners for 40 can be prepared in it. Giving it an illusion of grandeur are the mirrored backsplash and elegant hardware; efficiency factors include an electric cooktop that doubles as countertop and cabinetry designed to house specific gear, with hydraulic lifts to carry heavy appliances up and away when not in use, shelves all the way to the 10-foot ceiling, even drawers in the baseboards. There is an adjacent pantry that is home to the refrigerator.

9 WAYS TO MAKE THE MOST OF KITCHEN STORAGE

Kitchen storage should be convenient—include it as part of your overall set-up, not as an afterthought. Here are things to consider.

1.
ZONE YOUR KITCHEN. Assign every task and activity to a specific location. Decide which accoutrements belong in each zone and then figure out how to arrange them there.

2.
MEASURE EVERYTHING. Record the inside dimensions of cabinets, cupboards, and drawers so you can add storage devices that fit them efficiently.

3.
PULLOUT STORAGE WORKS WONDERS. Whether drawers and sliding shelves are part of your cabinets or inserts you add, they make it easy to access the back of a storage space.

4.
DISPLAY GREAT GEAR. If you have handsome copper pans or colorful mixing bowls, don't stash them; give them a prominent place in the kitchen.

5.
BE REALISTIC. If you have a small kitchen, admit it and don't expect it to accommodate banquet equipment.

6.
DIVIDE AND CONQUER.
- Add drawer dividers; use stacking bins and wire or plastic shelves in larger cabinets.
- Group same-size jars so they fit side-by-side neatly.
- Be imaginative—a cutlery tray may be the perfect thing for your spices.
- Use vertical dividers to separate lids, racks, baking sheets.
- It's fine to nest bowls and baking dishes as long as you can access them easily.
- Screw cup hooks under shelves, or add a hanging system for stemware.
- Get a rack for boxed food wraps.
- Invest in stackable food storage containers—they'll keep your fridge neater.

7.

USE THE WALL SPACE. Hanging storage is convenient and can be very attractive. Incorporate wire grid, rack, or bar systems for utensils and pans. Many of these systems can be fitted with shallow shelves and baskets for condiments, lids, cookbooks, or even a pot of herbs.

8.

TRASH HAPPENS. Make a plan for your garbage and recyclables from the outset. Home supply stores have slide-out trash can supports you can add to your base cabinets.

9.

WEIGHTY MATTERS. Put heavy things in lower cabinets.

Flooring requires a trade-off—porcelain tiles are inexpensive and durable but hard on your feet; WOOD IS SOFT TO WALK ON but requires more maintenance.

Sleek warmth. Stainless steel and black granite have an industrial strength that's softened when mixed with warm cherry wood. The handsome bar counter appears to float, a nice touch since it's viewed from an adjacent larger living space.

Masterful layout. A generous U-shape layout provides lots of storage and work space in a minimal area. This one opens above the base cabinets, lets the cook be part of the party, and serves as a pass-through.

Partial view. Consider creating an interior window to link kitchen and dining areas without actually merging them. This one opens above the kitchen counter, lets guests chat with the cook, and facilitates serving.

Good connection. In an open floor plan, a half-height wall offers a way to define and bring light to a windowless interior kitchen. This one is tall enough to hide the counter on the kitchen side and serve as a breakfast bar or extra workstation. The wraparound corner at the right end of the counter adds display space to the adjacent room.

Fluorescent lighting makes a kitchen look cold and austere, like an operating room. It's your home— keep the lighting WARM AND INVITING.

Graphic accent. Cabinetry with inset doors, shelves seen through glass, open storage cubes, and a tile backsplash compose a variety of grid patterns on these walls. The ocean-blue glass tiles and slate countertop provide a restful focal point between the mix of gleaming stainless-steel and glass and the rich, honey-hued wood cabinets.

Simple sophisticate. Wood and stainless steel combine to give this compact kitchen a sleek, modern feel. It's efficiently designed, with the appliances close to the island workspace. Guests can sit at the island while the host prepares dinner.

10 DETAILS THAT MAKE A SMALL KITCHEN GREAT

1.

TASK LIGHTING. Recessed lights beneath hanging cabinets provide vital focused illumination for working at the counters below, especially if windows are lacking.

2.

PLATE RACK. This is a good storage trick for a space-deprived kitchen. It adds a great look, and you won't have to open a cabinet every time you need a plate.

3.

CROWN MOLDING. Molding at the wall and ceiling joint adds a polished finish and can make a room feel bigger.

4.

CABINET DOORS. Mix solid-panel and glass-front cabinet doors to create a focal point: The eye tends to sweep past solid doors and go straight to the glass-front ones.

5.

EAT-IN KITCHEN. In an apartment, having more than just one place to eat makes the overall habitat feel more spacious. Try to find a nook or cranny where you can squeeze in a small countertop and several stools.

6.

DISPLAY SPACE. A glass shelf installed near the top of a window can show off a collection without blocking the light. Top cabinets with pretty bowls, pitchers, or vases.

7.

DEEP SINK. Instead of a wide sink, opt for a deep one. You'll gain counter space and find it easier to fill large pots.

8.

COLORS. Work out a color scheme by finding one thing in the kitchen that you love and then coordinate other items with it—using the same color family for all.

9.

APPLIANCE CAMOUFLAGE. Install a custom panel to conceal the dishwasher so that your small space won't be overwhelmed by a solid wall of appliances.

10.

CUSTOM CABINETS. If your budget allows for it, have custom cabinets designed and installed—they'll make the best use of every inch of your kitchen.

Tiny and tidy. Attention to detail makes up for lack of space in this miniscule kitchenette. The petite basin is fitted with a tall faucet to accommodate deep pans or vases, the two-burner cooktop is flanked with a modicum of counter, the skirt takes less space to open than cabinet doors, and the colors are restful.

Charmer. Good design solutions may lie hidden in quirky architectural details. Here, stepped masonry from a chimney provides graduated shelving, a charming backdrop for a tiny prep area. The curtain hides under-sink storage where a cabinet wouldn't fit, and the projecting countertop sneaks in a bit more work surface.

Dine in. An eat-in kitchen doesn't get much better than this—French doors pour light on dining and cooking areas; tiled wainscoting and floor remind us this is a workspace; and the round pedestal table and bentwood chairs are visually light, easy to walk around, and commodious.

Checkered floors should be painted or laid on the diagonal, which MAKES THE SPACE LOOK LARGER than a grid that's square to the walls.

Dish display. A display of great looking dishes makes a perfect backdrop to a table and chairs in a large kitchen. This sideboard offers handsome storage as well as a surface for serving, the open wall shelf balances lightly above it. The wire chairs and table pedestal keep the look airy.

Subtle contrast. Blue-gray subway tiles fill the wall space between counter and upper cabinets in this small kitchen, adding quiet distinction to the otherwise all-white space. The stylized paisley window shade is in keeping with the ethnic textile patterns used throughout the apartment.

Cook's classic. In this superbly organized kitchen, cooks are fortunate to have lots of work, storage, and foot space. Smaller rooms that are similarly filled will seem expansive if they borrow the pale colors, good lighting, and reflective surfaces of this design.

bathrooms

Sparkling, relaxing yet energizing, comfortable, private. Your list of ideal bathroom attributes might also include luxurious, romantic, airy, and easy to maintain. You may be yearning for a spa, wishing for a space big enough for a double shower, or simply want never again to see the aged tile in your classic tub-shower. Your dreams and plans may be based on purely aesthetic goals—to have a bathroom that's beautiful in a way the one you've got is not; or driven by physical conditions—deterioration caused by water or age. Or a mix of both may be your excuse—a desire for more attractive fixtures, better lighting, or an improved layout as well as a need for a facelift of paint, caulk, or ventilation system.

Because they are regularly suffused with steam, the recipients of splashes and drips, and home to damp towels, bathrooms are challenging in the best of circumstances, and thus successful bathroom design is part aesthetics and part practicality. If you live in an older building, you may have a bathroom with wonderful period charm and ample proportions that you want to preserve, yet be faced with deteriorating surfaces or

Summer sky. Blue Celeste marble cladding the walls in this master bath evokes clouds and sky in a subtle use of pattern that feels modern. A large mirror on the wall above the tub reflects the window and grooming areas at the opposite end of the room and imparts an illusion of spaciousness.

fixtures and inadequate lighting; if your building is new you may find the bathroom bland or unpleasantly cold and sterile. Unless your bath has been recently updated, it's not surprising if you find it in need of anything from new paint to a complete renovation.

Whatever your goal for your bathroom, even if you are redecorating or renovating for entirely cosmetic reasons, you want to be sure the update will solve whatever problems you have with your current setup and wear well. To get off to a good start, answer the basic questions given in the Introduction—they'll help you evaluate whether the physical and financial challenges of altering plumbing, fixtures, and wiring are a wise undertaking for your particular situation as a renter or an owner.

Once you determine the appropriate scope for the job ahead, it's time to pull together your thoughts and ideas and plan the details. Begin by listing your goals and noting the particular challenges or problems you want to overcome. Apartment bathrooms often lack good ventilation, natural light, or adequate storage—is this the case for yours and if so, is it feasible for you to add a window or a closet, or will you need another solution to the problem? Must you exchange a pedestal sink for a vanity in order to add storage? If you are on a budget, can you justify a marble tile floor if you install it yourself—and can you realistically do so?

To answer these questions and find inspiration, look through the photos in this chapter; flag the ones that appeal to you, including images of details as well as overall design. Also clip pictures of bathrooms you like from magazines or catalogs. Be open to clever ideas for lighting, layout, or storage even if their aesthetic is not the look you are after. And to make sure you plan a space that's efficient and attractive, read "8 Details that Make a Big Difference" and "Before You Soak or Pamper, Organize!" You'll find you are well on your way to your ideal bathroom.

Glamour puss. A daring mix of dark color and dressy furniture with traditional lines gives this small bathroom a comfortable elegance. Dark walls obscure boundaries to make a small space like this larger; a coating of liquid wax adds depth to this chocolate-color, complementing the formal bronze-and-marble vanity and setting off a chiseled 1950s mirror.

Place **BIG MIRRORS** opposite one another to enlarge a small bathroom.

Urbane individualist. Stone tiles covering nearly every surface, a huge mirrored cabinet, and frameless glass doors on the tub shower give this bath an austere sophistication. The sink counter is striking, with the faucet and controls mounted on the backsplash and a makeup station adjacent to the basin.

Just add chrome. This classic bath has been elegantly outfitted with handsome shower and basin controls, a neatly suspended curtain pole, and a graceful oversize sconce. The shiny wall surface and inset mirrored cabinet door make a sleek contrast to the cloth shower curtain and traditional fixtures.

8 DETAILS THAT MAKE A BIG DIFFERENCE

Many of the details that make a décor personal and pulled together are fairly easy to update but often overlooked. Getting them right can turn your apartment from anonymous to home, so cast an eye over these when you plan your space.

1.

HARDWARE. From cabinet handles and hinges to the knobs on your entry or interior doors, hardware is so functional and taken for granted that we often forget it has style. There are countless options and it's usually easy to change.

2.

MOLDINGS. Architectural detail at the ready: Chair rails, moldings, pilasters, and roundels may add elegance you covet or impose a look you can't abide. Depending on which, you can add them, remove them, highlight them with paint, or paint them over.

3.

COUNTERTOPS. It's relatively easy to replace countertops and doing so can give your kitchen or bathroom a great facelift even if you can't replace the cabinets.

4.

APPLIANCES. Updates are easy and only as costly as you wish. Consider surface (for both style and upkeep), cost of operating, and ambient noise, which may be surprisingly apparent in a small or open-plan apartment.

5.

FLOORING AND CARPETS. These add color and warmth; they can also add pattern— think tile, parquet, woven design. While replacing your flooring may be too big an undertaking, refinishing a wood floor or adding an attached carpet are both options. Area carpets or rugs can be moved when you do.

6.

FIXTURES AND FITTINGS. Tubs, sinks—even toilets—have style, and old, chipped or scratched ones are not an enhancement to your sense of well-being. Good looking faucets and controls make a huge difference; sometimes new ones are all it takes to update an older bathroom or kitchen.

7.

WALLCOVERINGS. Be it paint, wallpaper, or a textile, plain is always fine, but pattern may appeal to you. If you plan to redo, consider the scale of any pattern and whether you want to add sheen or incorporate a texture. Get a sample and look at it in different types of daylight and in lamplight.

8.

WINDOW TREATMENTS. Regardless of their decorating style, most apartment dwellers need window coverings that provide privacy. Even if you eschew curtain panels or fancy swags, include opaque, adjustable shades or blinds in your plan— they'll virtually disappear when raised.

An **UNDERMOUNTED SINK** makes as much sense in a bathroom vanity as it does in the kitchen—counter cleanup is easy.

Artistic ambiance. An eye-catching painting dominates this bath, where a custom-made marble surround on the soaking tub and elegant console basin mix with a tall mirror and whimsical pendant lights to create a pleasant blend of Old World and modern aesthetics.

Beauty at the ready. There's always a pretty face in the mirror of this retro bathroom. Whimsy aside, the small painted bureau provides needed storage and counter space and, with glass knobs and top tiled to match the tiles on the wall, feels right at home.

Blue surround. A frameless glass shower enclosure and large mirror on the wall amplify the proportions of this bathroom. Contrasting but coordinated tile on the floor and tub and shower surrounds introduces color; the large shower includes ceiling-mounted and hand-held showerheads.

Spectacular. A large photograph on glass inset in the wall above the tub creates the illusion of a window where none exists in this master bath. All-white Thassos marble and an efficient layout set off the vibrant "view."

Spiritual refuge. Contrasting matte and shiny surfaces, spacious layout, and clean lines form the calm and soothing structure of this bathroom. A large glass shower enclosure takes advantage of the expanse of windows, allowing natural light to flood the entire room. Floating in the center of the shower, where it creates a sculptural focal point, is a cast-concrete tub on a concrete slab. The custom console-style vanity is made of nickel and mahogany, and topped with the same honed limestone used for the floor and walls.

Integrated space. Frameless glass separates the shower from the rest of this bathroom without diminishing the overall space or impeding the light from the large window. There is no threshold, and the stone-tiled floor flows without interruption throughout; a window seat encourages relaxation in the shower.

Pure drama. Sand-colored Persian limestone forms a neutral box for this large shower, where the back wall, made of single massive slab of rare Nero Portoro marble, works as a gorgeous piece of art. An unobtrusive rain showerhead in the ceiling ensures a luxurious stream of water.

Paneled panache.
Custom woodwork creates a rich, warm environment in this bath. The vanity is extra-deep to permit the built-out mirror with small storage cubbies up the sides; the long-arm sconce ensures that light reaches the mirror.

Dapper stripes.
Large square tiles, in two tones of terra-cotta, stripe the walls in an unusual application that provides a strong, graphic background for this bathroom. The wall-mounted sink features a small, very convenient, integral counter.

Well groomed. A panel of small, richly colored brown tiles set with pale grout forms a strong frame behind this wall-mounted sink and plain mirror, and adds an element of verticality to the small room.

Understated. This classic all-white bath gets a boost from the contemporary lamp on the wall above the framed mirror (which is the medicine cabinet door). Whether period or brand new, a glass shelf on metal brackets is an asset where there is neither vanity nor counter.

Twice as nice. Golden glazed walls and an interesting, counter-mounted lamp give this thoroughly modern basin alcove a warm glow. The glass basin sits atop a stone counter, the water control is mounted on the mirror, which, of course, doubles the effect of each accoutrement.

BEFORE YOU SOAK
OR PAMPER, ORGANIZE!

START WITH A REALITY CHECK:

· How many people share the bathroom?
· What must you store there?
  And what is optional?
· Are there built-in cupboards,
  or is freestanding storage a possibility?

GOOD DESIGN HELPS BANISH CLUTTER:

· If your bathroom looks attractive you'll be more likely to keep it tidy, so even if you are outfitting a small bath or working with a low budget it makes sense to keep an aesthetic eye on your organizing.
· A mishmash of bins and baskets never looks neat and will soon overflow.
· Towels, rugs, and robes that clash with the walls don't ask for respect.
· Accessories are easy to come by in catalogs and home stores, so survey the options and make a plan that looks good and solves your storage challenge.

HELP YOURSELF TO KEEP THINGS TIDY:

- Towel bars provide better drying surface than rings.
- Add-on cupboard organizers such as wire shelves, small divided bins, and caddies keep items separated and accessible and hold bottles upright.
- Install a medicine cabinet if none is there; put a lock on it to prevent small fry from playing with the contents.
- Stacking bins with drawers don't take much floor space and require no installation.
- Hanging shelf units often include handy drawers, hooks, or a towel bar.
- Slide an attractive étagère with open or closed storage over your toilet.
- Keep wastebaskets small and empty them often.
- Use a shower caddy—chrome wears better than coated wire.

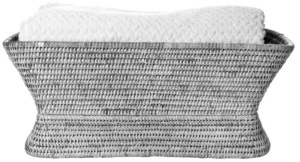

FIND ANOTHER HOME FOR THESE:

- Towels and linens—damp is the enemy of textiles so if possible, keep only towels currently in use in your bathroom.
- Bulk paper goods—if you have lots of closet space in your bathroom, fine; but otherwise, put paper products elsewhere or buy in smaller quantities.
- Cleaning supplies—sure, it's convenient to have them handy, but chemicals and mops don't mix with toiletries.

Fine indulgence. The long vanity in the room above and opposite was inspired by an office credenza. Made of zebrawood, it sits on short legs, is low, and topped by a slab of white marble. The exceptionally large rectangular vessel sink on top was chosen to compensate for the low height—bringing the vanity up to standard height for an under-mounted sink would have spoiled its credenza effect.

For the "me moments." Filled by a solid stream of water falling straight from the ceiling, this Japanese soaking tub sits high above Lake Michigan, with unbelievable views enhancing the luxurious, spacious, serene spa experience of time spent here. Reflecting the room is a wall of watery back-painted blue glass, which makes a person sitting in the tub feel like she's floating out over the lake.

bedrooms

Serene, secluded, comfortable, personal. Your ideal bedroom might also be airy, cozy, romantic, capacious, or spare. No matter its size or style, a bedroom should be a refuge, a private place designed to suit your needs and tastes. Sleep is probably its principal use, but as you plan its décor, think of what else you use your bedroom for—dressing room, office, library, craft studio—and accommodate whatever this might be. However you set it up, make sure there is good reading light—next to an easy chair, at the bedside, or both.

You may be blessed with a large and gracious bedroom or find yourself learning to love one that is tiny. If you live in a studio apartment, you lack the luxury of separation from the rest of your home and must either camouflage your bed or flaunt it. Whatever your situation, as an apartment dweller, privacy and quiet are probably issues for you, and closet space is likely one, too. Where there are nearby neighbors' windows or pedestrians, window treatments are a must; if there is ambient street light at night, you want light-blocking coverage even if your location is

Whimsy. Vivid hues used sparingly give a playful wake-up call to pastel walls and white linens. Hard geometry—the red chests, desk, and chair—contrasts with the sweet, bright details of the frilly curtains and floral upholstered headboard.

removed from straying eyes. Soundproofing, whether structural or added with carpets and draperies, will muffle sounds from neighboring quarters and the street—and tone down music, conversation, or feet pattering in other rooms of your own home. If closet space is tight, an armoire or bureau can supplement storage; but depending on your situation and the look you wish to live with, closet-organizing systems or built-in cupboards could be more effective solutions.

The style you choose for your bedroom is up to you—the décor can be as eccentric, overblown, or minimalist as you like. However, if you do spend a lot of waking time in the room, you may prefer a tailored look that makes you feel alert or professional to something romantic or sweet with a profusion of linens or distracting accessories. In a studio apartment it often makes sense to consider the "bedroom" furnishings as living room pieces, with a sofa bed, or a daybed dressed to be a sofa, and a chest of drawers that complements your other "public" accessories.

As you begin to pull your ideas together, review the basic questions in the Introduction—they'll help you assess the nature of the work ahead; and, especially if you are contemplating structural changes, they'll remind you to evaluate the undertaking for your situation as a renter or owner. Jot down your goals for your bedroom—are there problems you wish to solve, or is your chief interest a cosmetic makeover? Look through the photos in this chapter and flag the ones that appeal to you; be sure to flag any that provide solutions to challenges you face even if the décor isn't what you have in mind. Read the special features, "7 Tips for Making All-White Work," "Set Up a Closet That Works," and "8 Invaluable Uses for Textiles." Refine your plan, put it in motion, and look forward to sweet dreams.

Channel a grand room. In the spirit of great English bedrooms, an antique Coromandel screen, which cued the palette, frames a faux-horn bed with a tufted leather headboard and scallop-edged canopy.

Grownup pastels. A palette of saturated pastels in a mix of warm and cool hues gives a sophisticated edge to this bedroom. Although the color choices are pink, lavender, and pale blue, the modern furnishings and tailored linens swing the décor away from little-girl sweet to provide a softly sleek ambiance.

Clear and airy. These framed translucent panels make the best of a dearth of closets—angled rods projecting from the wall behind them hold clothes—while the size of the room appears undiminished. To minimize the distraction of the shadowy view of the contents, the owner has edited the front garments for consistent color and shape.

7 TIPS FOR MAKING ALL-WHITE WORK

Serene, elegant, pristine, cold, feminine, fresh, streamlined, summery, wintery, modern, sophisticated—white is a chameleon color that suits many decorating tastes. When thoughtfully composed, an all-white décor can be many things—just not noisy or boring.

1.
WHITE-ON-WHITE, BUT NOT PURE. White needn't be limited to a single hue. Ecru, ivory, beige, straw, dove, palest blush, blue and green tints, light natural wood tones, and antiqued and silvery metals all have a legitimate place in white-on-white décor.

2.
JUXTAPOSE TEXTURES. Combine sheers, nubby chenille, laces, airy mohair, matelassé, smooth percale and muslin.

3.
SHADOW IS ANOTHER KIND OF WHITE. Use white furnishings with sculptural details that cast, and catch, shadows: metal beds with ornamental fittings, woven wicker, painted pieces with carved moldings, ceramics with raised details, knobs, and handles, ruffled curtains or slipcovers with gathered skirts or sashes tied in bows, crocheted throws. Arrange white crockery in a white open cupboard.

4.
FIND NUANCE IN LAYERS. Tone-on-tone effects come from peeling paint, light passing through sheer fabrics on windows or furniture, a layer of lace over a solid cloth, mirrored reflections, walls painted with a ragged, strié, or cerused technique, and piles of pillows on a bed.

5.
LET THE SUN SHINE IN. Natural daylight adds warmth. Both sunlight and moonlight make architecture and furnishings cast shadows, which add character.

6.
SIMPLE OR COMPLEX AS BEFITS THE STYLE. Stick with the furnishings appropriate to your décor: Don't add ruffles to a modern interior just because the window treatment is white, don't force chrome chairs into a Victorian dining room that's decked in muslin and lace.

7.
EXPLOIT THE CLEANNESS. An all-white décor is always refreshing in a bathroom and makes a kitchen look wholesome and efficient. The surface of the materials you choose can refine the mood and swing it from clinical to quaint.

Semi-private. A mix of sliding and swinging translucent glass panels makes an adjustable barrier between this bedroom and living room, allowing light and air to circulate and permitting privacy when desired. Note the large mirror that balances the window on the opposite side of the bed and visually opens the space still further.

Airy. While the rough brick floor and sloped ceiling distinguish this space from the everyday studio apartment, the use of the floor-to-ceiling sheer curtain to separate public and private areas without diminishing the space or light is a simple idea that anyone who lives in one room can borrow.

Bed-sitter. The clean lines of tailored upholstery and soft Roman shades combine with creamy tones and formal accessories to create a quiet bedroom that invites conversation, reflection, and relaxation. Windows and lamps ensure there is always good lighting at the loveseat.

Ensemble dressing. This bed is positioned away from the street but facing the view, and dressed to match the loveseat and window shades (seen above), with an upholstered headboard to complete the ensemble of furnishings.

Grand illusion. Reflected here in a huge framed mirror, the full-length curtains covering the wall on each side of the window make a cocoon-like backdrop for the bed and give the illusion of additional windows behind them. A leaning mirror of this scale tricks the eye into perceiving its frame as a doorway to rooms beyond.

Soothing hues. Sleek furnishings, a mix of seascape colors, and a variety of materials keep this bedroom calm and quiet. The iridescent silk that upholsters the walls changes under differing light conditions, going from blue to green with a subtle movement like sunshine and shadow playing on ocean waves.

Creamy refuge. Glamorous and comfortably plush, this bedroom is grounded with generous dark accents that contrast the otherwise creamy palette. The high bed with its tall curvy headboard makes you think the small room is larger than it is—small-scale furniture tends to keep a small space small. Unusual alabaster tulip lamps with "lots of personality" sit on the gold-accented black bedside chests.

BEFORE AND AFTER

Goodbye to Gloom

BEFORE

The symmetry of paired casement windows at one end of this bedroom was spoiled by an air conditioner, and their proportions distorted by the remnant of a cornice that must have topped curtains at one time. Tattered window shades and worn wallpaper completed the bleak décor.

AFTER

The windows assumed their rightful proportions among pilasters and soffits as soon as the cornice was removed. White paint gives a clean, serene background and the windows, now dressed with discreet white shades, are free to flood the room with daylight.

1. The jazzy overhead fan keeps the air pleasantly circulating in all seasons.

2. A simple, custom-made headboard, upholstered in soft chenille, centers the bed on the plain wall.

3. A small, wall-mounted lamp with a flexible arm provides good reading light; its switch is within arm's reach so there's no need to leave the bed to turn it off.

4. An easy chair in front of the windows takes advantage of the room's length as well as its light; there is plenty of space for a sitting area.

5. Paired low bedside tables are generously sized to hold books, flowers, water, coffee, or whatever accoutrements are needed.

Wake up to springtime. Grass-green and white make morning in this room fresh and bright on even the gloomiest winter day. Contrasting large patterns bring drama to the small space, where the tension of bold striped curtains against the curvy patterned damask lining the walls has the effect of architecture outdoors against a leafy bower.

Background check. Brick walls provide a softly patterned, textured backdrop that makes a surprising complement to this eclectic collection of Asian and contemporary furnishings. The key to finding things that work? Each piece must be visually strong enough not to be swallowed by the walls. Plus here, the rug mutes the bold contrast of the dark floor.

Use pillows to add something different to a room—a splash of color, A GRAPHIC PATTERN, or some texture.

Perpetual sunshine. Brilliant yellow walls intensify the radiance of the morning sun, whose warmth is echoed as well by the sham and matelassé coverlet and tempered, ever so slightly, by white sheers at the window.

Room to grow up. Hip and young, with splashes of modern art, this bedroom suits a teen now and will keep its appeal as she grows up. It's inviting and not too serious, with graphic accents on the extra-high headboard and Roman shade, blocks of vivid lavender, playful art, and ethnic print pillows mixing with a slightly funky, navy patent-leather chair.

BEFORE AND AFTER | Bold Strokes on a Small Scale

AFTER

The owner felt she might as well flaunt what she didn't have, and opted to make the small space lively. Possessing an excellent eye for design, she looked for one bold gesture that would transform her room, and decided to exploit her love of red by using it everywhere—as an accent—to unite her jumbled furnishings. The result is an individual décor with unmistakable passion and new comfort.

1. A single pair of curtains spans the end wall—they minimize the off-center focus, take less space than two pairs, and are trimmed with red ribbon.

2. A shocking pink Parsons table doubles for desk and dining. The glossy scarlet lampshade atop a swirling glass base provides light.

3. Thick cushions have transformed the radiator covers into window seats—a great way to accommodate guests in a room where there's barely space for a single easy chair.

4. The armoire has been moved across the room for a more comfortable fit.

5. Red-and-white textiles in assorted patterns and small amounts enliven various furnishings—plaid on the ottoman, ticking stripe on the headboard and for the armoire curtains, toile for a bench and chair.

BEFORE

This tiny room comprises most of the space in a small walk-up apartment and must serve for living, dining, and sleeping. A regimented arrangement of white furnishings with neutral accents kept the space as open as possible, but was bland and looked cluttered rather than composed. Off-center windows added to the challenge.

Happy hues. Brightly colored accessories enliven a decorating scheme, especially when set against lots of white. They can be fun and eye-catching—or overwhelming. Here the sharp contrast of hot orange against white is beautifully balanced by a cool blue kimono sprayed with orange flowers.

Pure crème fraîche. Walls the color of heavy cream and a white Berber carpet set the stage for a deliciously feminine bed, which has a headboard upholstered in ivory mohair and froufrou curtains in soft melon tones. Off to the side, a fuchsia-velvet Louis XV chair adds pop.

White motif. A ceiling-mounted pole allows this ell to be curtained-off from the adjacent living room. The white, ring-topped curtains match those at the far window, ensuring that the décor is unified at all times, from all angles.

SOFT LAYERS ARE ROMANTIC—add more pillows, lace, and throws if that's the look you're after.

Alcove illusion. A panel of gathered, sheer white fabric suspended from a ring hung high above the bed makes a tent-like enclosure—ethereal here from sunlight flooding through the window at the head of the bed.

Collector's haven. In this spacious, airy bedroom, light walls and an earthy palette are the underpinnings to a mix of furnishings, textiles, and objects collected by an inveterate traveler. Covering the carved bed is an antique sari; the various objects on display are grouped (but not lined up) for impact.

Cozy contrast. Dark walls bring intimacy to this mezzanine sleeping area, which, being open to the stairs and floor below on one side, could feel rather exposed. The honey-colored ceiling, carpet, and throw, and sepia-tone prints in gold frames preclude any sense that the dark is closing in on you.

Artful repose. Go for dark walls to make a sleeping space restful—something to consider if ambient city lights filter into your bedroom. Here, deep chocolate makes a fitting background for tailored linens, spare furnishings, and a display of arresting graphics.

Satisfyingly graphic. Make black and white symmetrical and the effect
is especially crisp, clean, and orderly. Here, a black upholstered headboard
extends behind the white bed and chests in a modern take on wainscoting; yellow
lampshades add a grace note.

Casually refined. A symmetrical composition
of bed, writing table, and framed prints establishes
a formal framework that makes this bay-windowed
bedroom feel architectural and a little grand, which
allows smaller accessories to be scattered around
comfortably, without looking messy.

Tableau. A symmetrical display of artwork helps to balance a bulky piece of furniture like a bureau, adding height without mass and keeping the bureau from looking lonely. Here, framed botanicals sit gently against the busy wallpaper; the stepped arrangement encourages the eye to travel and take in each piece.

Centered display. The pretty mirror centered over this bureau is the hub for a display of framed botanicals. Placed opposite a window to reflect the cityscape, it gives the illusion of a portal through the interior wall.

Use MATCHING FRAMES for artwork that is part of a series. Change the frame scale if the artwork varies in size, but maintain the style.

SET UP A CLOSET
THAT WORKS

PROVIDE AN INFRASTRUCTURE. Closets that are well outfitted hold a lot more than you expect. So shop for your closet—there are many good organizing systems, some ready-made, some made to measure. For inspiration, check out the clothing displays in boutiques, you'll find good ideas for fitting lots of garments in a small space.

ANALYZE YOUR NEEDS AND THEN SET UP YOUR SPACE. The person who always dresses in jeans and tees has very different needs from the person who frequents the ballroom every weekend. Measure the space you need to store different kinds of garments. Consider:

- Cubbyhole storage keeps everything in view and you don't need space for yourself to stand while you pull out a drawer.
- Deep drawers may be good for handbags, but for clothing they're an invitation to rummage. Save them for pillows and towels.
- Store shirts folded in a bureau if you're short of hanging space.
- Use tiered rods for short garments (fold trousers over their hangers); allocate only the space you really need for longer dresses and coats.
- It's easier to find what you want if you separate your clothing by the occasion for which it's suited—business, casual, or evening, as well as by type—jackets, pants, skirts.
- Take advantage of tall ceilings with high shelves for infrequently used items.

MAKE IT EASY TO KEEP THINGS CLEAN AND SAFE.

- Carpet your closet floor to cut down on dust.
- Invest in zippered storage bags to keep out-of-season clothes dust-free.
- Use the right kind of hanger in the right size to support each garment.
- Keep shoes and boots in bags, boxes, or racks so you can easily vacuum the floor.
- Add a shelf or small table to hold jewelry or the contents of your pocket while you dress.

CREATE A DRESSING ROOM.

- Install a full-length mirror in or near your closet so you don't have to trek to the bathroom to check out your outfit.
- Install hooks so you can organize an outfit before putting it on or packing it.
- If your closet is large, keep an iron set up.

Good grid. This tall wooden folding screen, composed of square lattice panels, does more than take the place of a headboard. It's intriguing, adds texture, provides focus, takes up no space, requires little or no installation, and is portable—all excellent qualities for enhancing a bedroom that's small and architecturally unadorned or in a temporary residence.

Neat as a pin. Built-in, windowsill-height cabinets and a tall headboard bring architectural interest to a room that's otherwise plain. These cabinets provide a one-piece alternative to bureau, display shelves, and nightstand with no decision needed as to how best to arrange them.

8 INVALUABLE USES FOR TEXTILES

Textiles add dimension, texture, grace, color, and pattern. They can filter light or block it altogether. They soften floors, shed or absorb water, warm beds, and mask the undesirable. They're variously durable or ephemeral, precious or disposable. Available in nearly endless variety, they're simply invaluable as components of your décor. Choose them thoughtfully—balance style, durability, and budget—and put them to good use.

1.

DECORATIVE ACCESSORIES: Throw pillows, afghans and throws, table runners and toppers—these are small items that can be changed easily and add character to your furnishings. And if you're a textile lover, you'll include ethnic weavings, samplers, art quilts, and similar treasures you've collected to display as part of your décor.

2.

UPHOLSTERY AND SLIPCOVERS: Look for durable fabrics that feel good against your skin. Pets, children, sunlight, and spills all take a toll on fabric. Inexpensive furniture does not warrant a costly covering; good furniture is worth covering well.

3.

KITCHEN ACCESSORIES: Dish towels, aprons, potholders, place mats—choose styles that coordinate with your overall kitchen décor, but bear in mind the heavy use these items get and make sure they are washable.

4.

BATH LINENS: Good ones last for years, so let yourself splurge a bit. Be sure to include hand towels for guests in your collection.

Rugs are one of the **EASIEST WAYS** to introduce color. A strong rug adds depth and drama to a neutral space, a pale rug calms a lively space.

5.

RUGS AND CARPETS: May be flat weave or pile, patterned or plain, and come doormat to room-size—use them to accent or anchor accordingly.

6.

WINDOW TREATMENTS: Fabric type and construction style go hand-in-hand to create formal or casual window fashions. Look in books and magazines for ideas you'd like to live with. Catalogs and home centers offer myriad ready-made and semi-custom options. Make sure you account for your privacy needs when planning.

7.

DINING LINENS: Both casual and formal tablecloths and napkins are a must for most people. Make sure you know your table size when shopping. Stain-resistant finishes are an option to consider.

8.

BED COVERINGS: Sheets, shams. blankets, quilts, duvet covers, throws, bed skirts and hangings—stylish options abound; custom fabrication is an option if you've something specific in mind.

Indulge your inner romantic. Canopied and elaborately turned, this four-poster frame invites sweet dreams in a room-within-a-room. It's big, but that's the point, especially since it must hold its own against bold patterns on the wall and upholstery and at the window.

Linger a while. A delicate, metal four-poster frame, dressed with neither canopy nor hangings, provides a sense of enclosure yet permits enjoyment of all the light and air present in this room; a great device where the ceiling is especially high and the windows very tall with a pretty topper.

Color forms. Here, a great use of color and thoughtful composition rescue the requisite bed, side tables, lamps, and blank wall from boredom. The arrangement is a good reminder that a balanced design need not be perfectly symmetrical.

Sleeping compartment. Little more than a hallway, this sleeping area connects the foyer and living area in a small studio apartment. The furniture, while simple, is dressy, decorative, and not overtly "bedroomy." The bed's high headboard and footboard provide a sense of enclosure and privacy—nice since the foot is adjacent to the living area.

A daybed with high headboard and footboard becomes A ROOM WITHIN A ROOM—perfect for a studio apartment.

Mirror as art. A tall mirror next to this bed frames a reflection of the hall and living room like a large, graphic painting—a fitting complement to the bold polka-dot rug and the intense blue panel at the head of the bed.

Light reflections. This large round mirror, set in an elliptical frame and centered above the bed, reflects ambient light. Absent anyone crossing the foot of the bed, it shows the opposite blank wall, appearing transparent and giving the sculptural frame its due. Note the extended upholstered headboard and divided chenille bedcover.

foyers, libraries, and offices

Exquisite extra or essential element—anyone would covet an apartment that includes a foyer or a room that can be dedicated to a library or office. If yours does not, you can create space within another room to satisfy your need for a place to drop your hat, store your books, or situate a desk. Large or small, such spaces should be designed to look great and facilitate the way you use them.

A foyer offers an immediate welcome in your home; if your apartment has a substantial entry hall, make the most of it. If not, even a small corner or hallway can be made inviting—a gloomy entry doesn't herald a warm home. Provide soft lighting, a place to put the mail and your handbag or briefcase, and decorate the space in a style that introduces the rest of your apartment.

Wow factor. Handpainted wallpaper of a type more often chosen for a dining room turns this entryway into an instant garden. Complementing the effect are a chevron floor, stained in contrasting colors to play up its bold geometry, and crystal orbs on the table, which add an "English cabinet-of-curiosities" feeling.

Libraries and office space are luxuries that some of us can't do without—if you fall into this group, you'll either choose an apartment because it provides the necessary space, or you'll find a way to accommodate your bookshelves or desk (or both) in your living or dining room, in your bedroom, or even in a hall closet.

Perhaps you are planning a major renovation, and if so, you can create the spaces you need. Maybe you live in a loft, where your foyer is simply the wall next to the entry door, and freestanding cupboards or shelves establish your library, or sliding panels create an office zone. If your quarters are more conventional, your plans will depend on how much space you can designate for these specific functions.

Apartment foyers often lack windows; office and library space can be carved from a passageway or tucked into a closet—both situations are plagued by a lack of natural light and fresh air. Whatever your situation, your needs are probably quite personal, so assess them honestly: Is your foyer really a mudroom? Or will it be your art gallery? Must your desk be behind doors? Will you need a ladder because your bookshelves stretch to the ceiling? How many people use the space? Can you afford custom-made or will you opt for furnishings from a home store or catalog? What are your requirements for wiring, cable and phone connections, and storage? If your space is to be multipurpose, what is the best overall aesthetic? How can you separate or combine the needed components?

Look through the photos in this chapter for good ideas and great design for foyers, library spaces, and offices. Go shopping to see the variety of furnishings available. Whatever your needs, begin your planning by reviewing the basic questions in the Introduction. They'll help you determine the scope of your project and whether it makes sense for you as a renter or owner. Read the special feature, "9 Steps to Clutter Control," for ways to impose order on the contents of your space. Pull together your ideas, make a plan, and put it to work.

Feel-good color. Vivid yellow splashes happily over these walls, bringing sunshine to a small, windowless foyer. The bold painting is balanced and visually anchored by a graceful painted side table, which is large enough to hold a few accessories but not so large you can't easily walk past it.

Reader's corner. Quirky spots like this small landing can provide just the space required for a collection of favorite volumes and a comfortable chair. It makes sense to devote precious floor space to bookshelves when there isn't enough area for a real room anyway, and the cozy décor invites a good read.

Industrial complex. A plastered niche is the focal point in this expanse of brick. It hosts a chest of drawers and artwork. In a repurposed industrial loft, it matters not that the intercom, fuse box, and electric conduits are exposed next to it.

Step Through a Gracious Entry

AFTER

With the railing, wainscoting, and wallpaper gone, and the step now spanning the full width of the opening, the transition between the foyer and living space is gracious and seamless even though a dining area now backs onto the step. White paint on walls and ceilings in both spaces makes each seem a logical, inviting extension of the other.

BEFORE

An awkward step and graceless metal railing were unwelcoming and blocked the flow of traffic between this foyer and the adjacent room. Fussy wallpaper made this entry gloomy and was a poor companion to the border hiding under the aged finish on the parquet floor.

1. A wall of custom-built bookshelves was artfully tucked next to the structural pilaster dividing the spaces.

2. In the foyer, the owner opted for a long, low cabinet that could hide running shoes and serve as a bench for donning them. It conceals shopping totes and other hallway necessaries as well.

3. The new step—a wide maple slab—appears to float across the opening. It is supported on conical feet installed tip-down and inset far enough to be nearly invisible.

4. Cleaned to reveal its original Art Deco pattern, the parquet floor gives a glorious accent to the apartment's modern furnishings.

Sophisticated entrance. Here's a fresh twist on the convention of lining a foyer with scenic wallpaper: A rhythmic pattern of large vines rising into the air is handpainted on the walls, making this interior hall feel light, airy, and ethereal. Extending the alfresco theme are the green lacquer garden seat and lattice-motif rug.

Niche potential. An architectural niche provides an empty frame begging to be filled. This one is just deep enough to hold a small sideboard and sports a tight arrangement of brightly framed graphics.

Book nook. An awkward angle is here put to good use housing a small bookcase, keeping it out of the way but handy to the nearby worktable. A collection of small photo portraits is whimsically tacked to the wall above.

Go modular. The composition of modules surrounding the doorway between the dining and living rooms provides open and closed storage and display space in this apartment. The unit is attractive, efficient, requires only a moderate area relative to its capacity, and extends neatly into the small adjacent hallway.

Aim for the rafters. A wall of shelves built floor-to-peak into the gable end of this room creates recessed doorways and lots of book space. White paint keeps the overall effect airy even though there's plenty on display. Somewhere a ladder stands ready to fetch objects from high shelves.

Impromptu. Grommeted canvas panels provide an informal background (and grand Roman shades) for the light-filled office in this garden apartment. The panels, along with the area rug, leaning painting, and freestanding shelves, are aesthetically appealing options for furnishing quarters that don't warrant physical repairs or built-in décor.

Double duty. This antique farm table serves as desk in a studio apartment, but when guests come for dinner, the crated accessories are quickly moved aside so it can be set for dining. The large mirror leaning against the wall reflects light and the view to make the space seem larger.

Totally booked. A classic library table placed in the middle of this small room leaves all the walls clear for book storage and enables the sitter to face the windows. Two floor lamps and one on the desk make the space bright at any hour.

Study hall. Making the most of this narrow passage, a desk is recessed between a bank of cabinets and a high wall; a spin of the chair takes you to the wall of modular shelves and drawers behind it. This corridor is open at the end to receive ambient light from the windows in the adjacent room, yet feels private even though it has no doors.

WHEN SPACE IS TIGHT, make sure your chair will push under the desk—you want an office, not an obstacle course.

Closet works. A wide closet fitted with shelves, a counter, and file cabinet makes a neat guest-room office that disappears behind bi-fold doors when company comes to stay. The wood paneled interior of this one makes it feel professional and intentional—not makeshift.

9 STEPS TO CLUTTER CONTROL

To some, clutter is anything that does not enhance our life on a regular basis. To others, it's anything, no matter how much we love it, that lands inappropriately on the kitchen table. Here are some tips for keeping both types in check.

1.

COLOR COORDINATE. Harmonize spaces by choosing accessories with a shared palette; this helps both small accoutrements, like pencil caddies, and larger ones, like picture frames or cushions and throws, to create a neat look when grouped.

2.

CLIMB THE WALLS. Use floating shelves to hold photos or books over desk, credenza, or buffet. Create vertical interest with shelves extending nearly to the ceiling to display collections or house your library.

3.

INVITE TIDINESS. Provide a basket for the mail, a bowl for keys, a tray for wet boots, a rack for hats—whatever it takes to fight the in-the-door-drop-it syndrome.

4.

INVEST IN ORDER. Purchase whatever organizing gear is right for you—from hanging folders for your file cabinet, to drawer dividers, to magazine bins and cardboard storage bins. If they won't be hidden, go for good looking. Label them, if appropriate, so you can identify the contents.

5.

DISCARD WITH DISCIPLINE. Put junk mail through the shredder or into the recycling bin as soon as it arrives. Three days is it for newspapers, and magazines go when the next edition arrives.

Furnishings that trick the eye by taking **LESS VISUAL SPACE** make a room seem uncluttered. Go for glass table tops, Lucite chairs or tables, and mirrors; paint bookshelves or built-in cupboards to match the walls.

6.

LOVE IT OR LEAVE IT. Require your possessions to defend themselves: If you neither love it nor use it, toss it.

7.

DISPLAY AND ENJOY IT. Forget stuffing your hat collection into the closet or your wooden spoons into the utensil drawer. Find a distinctive rack for the former and an appealing jug for the latter and declare them part of the décor.

8.

DOUBLE DUTY. Choose furniture that multitasks—an ottoman to double as seating and occasional table (and ideally as storage too); a coffee table with a shelf for magazines; a cupboard that can be topped with your collection of pitchers or bowls.

9.

HIDEAWAY. If it isn't attractive, conceal it. Opt for bookcases with doors and occasional tables with drawers.

Before you design your SMALL OFFICE SPACE, make a list of all the things you need to fit into it. Shop for furnishings that will hold them efficiently.

Back office. In small quarters, pushing a table against the sofa back may be the best way to build an office. Your workspace will be defined but still public; this one bridges the live/work challenge with a neat array of understated desk accoutrements and a trio of potted herbs.

Geek chic. Sometimes the edge of a mezzanine or stairwell offers just the right space for a small desk. A setup like this may be best for people who live alone or work when no one else is home.

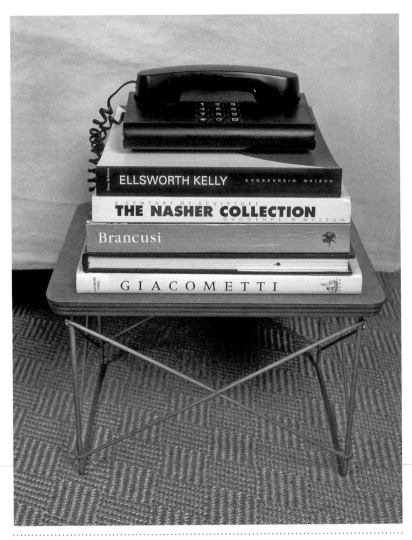

Land line. A stack of books adds height to this low end table and puts the phone within easy reach.

Keep it personal. Lots of small containers keep this tabletop desk organized despite a lack of drawers. The pretty lamp gives a soft, personal touch—perfect for a home office that doesn't want to be corporate.

Go retro. A small desk with light, streamlined proportions works for correspondence and doesn't take much space. The two-tiered top of this table provides a storage platform for papers or home for a keyboard without the bulky appearance of drawers.

If you have no other space available, let your DINING TABLE double as a desk; a low-hanging light will provide the best illumination.

Board room. When space is tight, place a long, narrow table against the wall to do double duty as desk and sideboard; add an attractive lamp that suits both roles. Bins tucked below this table keep books or stacked papers out of the way but within easy reach.

Yours truly. Ornate Asian cabinets provide a focal point for this small office and pass their colors on to the contemporary chairs and desk. Framed photos and stacks of books and periodicals vie for wall space under the sloped ceiling—this room is eclectic, personal, and inviting.

Independent study. Two steps up and sliding translucent panels set the home office apart in this spacious apartment. Note the counter-height perimeter shelves for extra work or storage space, the interior window that connects to the kitchen beyond, and the beautiful, bordered parquet floor.

photography credits

William Abranowicz: 84–85, 123; Lucas Allen: 70–71, 99; Christopher Baker: 133, 147 top; Tim Beddow: 20, 23, 119, 190, 222 top left, 265; Fernando Bengoechea: 67 top right, 153, 167; Antoine Bootz: 80, 116, 159, 205, 239; Jonn Coolidge: 14 left, 15, 69 (both photos), 72, 73, 90, 92, 102, 223, 224; Corbis: Fernando Bengoechea/Beateworks: 66; Roger Davies: 30, 31, 122, 142, 219, 257; Carlos Domenech: 139 left; Colleen Duffley: 221; Pieter Estersohn: 100, 129, 136–137, 165, 169, 207, 210, 217; Dana Gallagher: 68, 135, 272; Oberto Gili: 36, 158, 170, 193, 232, 256; Tria Giovan: 24–25, 27, 77, 114, 118, 138, 139 right, 161, 196, 197; Mick Hales: 44 top left, 45, 148, 149, 179, 225; John M. Hall: 62, 247, 258, 260; Christopher Irion: 134; iStockphoto: Kevin Link: 9; Meliden: 56; J. Horrocks: 124; Joe Brandt: 152; Thibault Jeanson: 54–55, 78, 79, 91, 204, 213, 228, 242–243; John Kernick: 184, 185; Francesco Lagnese: 255; Thomas Loof: 18–19, 34–35, 37 top right, 40–41, 48–49, 101, 104, 130, 155, 172, 177, 234, 249; Peter Margonelli: 53, 58–59, 94, 95, 112, 150, 166, 180, 181, 233; Kerri McCaffety: 108–109, 218; Joshua McHugh: 89; James Merrell: 13, 60, 96, 162, 189, 227 top; Peter Murdock: 63, 103, 151, 173, 178 right, 230, 252; Ngoc Minh Ngo: 6, 10, 105, 160; Brendan Paul: 244; Victoria Pearson: 22, 127, 128, 171, 200–201, 211, 214–215; David Phelps: 87; Eric Piasecki: 21, 28, 29 (both photos), 57, 64, 65, 113, 120, 121, 144–145, 147 bottom left, 229; Laura Resen: 125, 250–251, 261, 262; Eric Roth, 16, 17, 51, 61, 115, 117; Nathan Schroder: 43; René Stoeltie: 93; Tim Street-Porter: 46, 47, 156, 178 left, 216, 238; Tara Striano: 50, 74, 75, 111, 140, 141, 202, 203, 208, 209, 231, 240, 241, 263; Studio D: Lara Robby: 182 top left and right, 183, 226 (all photos), 254 left; Philip Friedman: 227 bottom; Jan Tham: 157, 194, 246; Domonique Vorillon: 38, 82, 83, 182 bottom left, 191, 212, 245; William Waldron: 88, 110, 248, 253; Björn Wallander: 186; Simon Watson: 206; Paul Whicheloe: 39, 106 left, 195 top right; Luke White: 76, 86, 220, 237, 259; Vicente Wolf: 32–33, 107, 143, 174–175, 176, 198, 199; Gaby Zimmermann: 81

Front Cover: James Merrell
Back Cover: Thomas Loof

index